Ludwig van Beethoven

Ludwig van Beethoven

MUSICAL GENIUS

BRENDAN JANUARY

FRANKLIN WATTS
A Division of Scholastic Inc.
New York Toronto London Auckland Sydney
Mexico City New Delhi Hong Kong
Danbury, Connecticut

Photographs © 2004: AKG-Images, London: 66 (Beethoven Haus, Bonn), 9 left, 76, 86; Art Resource, NY: 32 (Giraudon/Beethoven House, Bonn), 36 (Erich Lessing), 6, 50, 74, 95 (Eric Lessing/Beethoven House, Bonn), 45, 88 (Erich Lessing/Gesellschaft der Musikfreunde, Vienna), 53 (Erich Lessing/Helenental, Baden), 43, 56, 69, 72 (Erich Lessing/Historisches Museum der Stadt, Vienna, Austria), 48 (Erich Lessing/Museum, Troppau), 2 (Scala/Civico Museo Bibliografico Musicale Rossini, Bologna); Bridgeman Art Library International Ltd., London/New York: cover (Giraudon/Beethoven Haus, Bonn, Germany), 10, 25, 34 (Historisches Museum der Stadt, Vienna, Austria), 20 (Kunsthistorisches Museum, Vienna, Austria), cover background (Private Collection), 38 (Schloss Charlottenburg, Berlin, Germany); Corbis Images: 15, 27 (Archivo Iconografico, S.A.), 9 right (Bettmann), 96 (Hulton-Deutsch Collection), 61 (Royalty-Free); Hulton | Archive/Getty Images: 42 (Neil Libbert), 59, 82, 98; The Art Archive/Picture Desk: 17 (Dagli Orti/Museum der Stadt Wien).

Library of Congress Cataloging-in-Publication Data

January, Brendan.
    Ludwig van Beethoven : musical genius / by Brendan January.
        p. cm. — (Great life stories)
    Includes bibliographical references and index.
    ISBN 0-531-11909-2
    1. Beethoven, Ludwig van, 1770—1827—Juvenile literature.   2. Composers—Austria—Vienna—Biography—Juvenile literature.   I. Title. II. Series.
ML3930.B4J35 2004
780'.92-dc22

                                                                    2004006439

Printed in the United States of America.
1 2 3 4 5 6 7 8 9 10 R 13 12 11 10 09 08 07 06 05 04

Contents

This is a room in the house where Beethoven was born in Bonn. Today his childhood home is a museum.

Growth of a Musician

More than two hundred years ago, Ludwig van Beethoven was born in Bonn, a small city in Germany. Over the course of his life, Beethoven composed some of the most passionate and beautiful music ever written. Today, his works can be heard on numerous recordings and in crowded concert halls around the world.

When people need to express their emotions, they often turn to Beethoven's music. The opening notes of his Fifth Symphony were played to rally Allied resistance against the Nazis during World War II. The mournful, slow movement from his Third Symphony was played during the funeral procession for President John F. Kennedy in 1963. In 1989, the Berlin Wall, a symbol of oppression and a world divided by the cold war, came crashing down. An orchestra of musicians from several different nations gathered to play Beethoven's Ninth Symphony.

Some people may wonder how Beethoven composed such music. The answer to that question lies in Beethoven's fascinating life. Born into an unhappy household, shattered by deafness in middle age, Beethoven was often in a state of emotional turmoil. Beethoven was also born into a time when the social order was being violently upended by revolution. Swept up by his own emotions and the spirit of his times, Beethoven expressed the pain, joy, hope, and rage of the human experience in music.

CHILDHOOD IN BONN

Ludwig van Beethoven was born on December 16 or 17, 1770. His home, Bonn, was a peaceful city of about ten thousand people that sat on the Rhine River in Germany. The Beethovens were a musical family. Beethoven's grandfather, also named Ludwig, settled in Bonn in 1732. He was attracted to Bonn because it was the capital city of the surrounding area.

Beethoven's Germany

Beethoven was born and raised in an area that is part of Germany today. But during Beethoven's lifetime, Germany didn't exist. Instead, the region was a patchwork of states. Many of these states ruled themselves. Others were part of the vast Holy Roman Empire, which was dominated by the Hapsburg family of Vienna. Bonn was the capital of one of the regions ruled by the Hapsburgs.

The ruler of Bonn, called the elector, lived in a fine palace and held court. The rituals of the court demanded music for many occasions, such as marches, church masses, funerals, and, of course, dances and parties. Ludwig's grandfather became one of the elector's musicians.

Ludwig van Beethoven's father, Johann, also became a musician. In 1767, Johann van Beethoven married Maria Magdalena. Tragically, their first-born son died shortly after his birth in 1769. One year later, the couple had another boy, Ludwig van Beethoven.

Ludwig van Beethoven began his life in an unhappy household. His father, Johann, held a secure position as a singer at the court and gave private lessons on the piano and violin. These jobs earned him enough money to support his family comfortably. Johann, however, was fond of drinking. When he was not at home, Johann spent his time with friends in taverns, drinking and hanging out.

Ludwig's parents, Johann and Maria, had lost one child before the birth of Beethoven.

A NEW CHILD STAR?

Johann began to educate his son in music as soon as Ludwig could reach a piano keyboard. Soon, Ludwig played the piano with great skill. But Ludwig was not safe from the poisonous effect alcohol had on his father. Sometimes, long after everyone else was asleep, Ludwig's father stumbled into the household after a night of drinking. He pulled young Ludwig from his slumber and placed him, weeping, in front of the piano. "Play!" his father shouted. While his father hovered over him and listened for mistakes, Ludwig played the piano through his tears until dawn.

Considering his father's harsh teaching methods, it is amazing that the young Ludwig did not hate both the piano and music. Instead, Ludwig learned so quickly that Johann came up with an idea. More than ten years earlier, the young Wolfgang Amadeus Mozart had toured Europe, playing the piano before princes and wealthy audiences. He earned great acclaim and, more importantly to Johann, great amounts of money. Johann eagerly planned to introduce the world to yet another child prodigy. On March 26, 1778, Johann gave a

Ludwig spent part of his childhood touring and performing music.

concert that featured the young Ludwig on the piano. To impress the crowd, Johann advertised that Ludwig was only six years old. He was actually seven.

Ludwig's career as a child prodigy was short, however. Even at this young age, he resented performing "like a trained monkey." His concerts were successful for a short time, but then drew little attention.

A PAINFUL LIFE AT HOME

By this time, Ludwig van Beethoven had two younger brothers, Caspar Carl (born in 1774) and Nikolaus Johann (born in 1776). Even the addition of two more sons could not bring happiness to the Beethoven household. A neighbor observed that the children grew up dirty and unkempt. Johann continued to drink, and Ludwig's mother seemed unable to rise above her bitterness. She urged a friend, "If you want to take my good advice, remain single, and then you will have the most tranquil, most beautiful, most pleasurable life. For what is marriage? A little joy, but then a chain of sorrows." A neighbor observed that the "children were not brought up with gentleness; they were often left in charge of the maids. Their father was very strict with them."

Bewildered and confused by the painful situation at home, young Ludwig kept to himself. One classmate described Ludwig as withdrawn, ill-humored, and unable to hold a conversation. To make matters worse, Ludwig's school grades were miserable, and Johann was angered that his son appeared unable to learn anything.

Ludwig was learning, but not in the classroom or through conversations with friends. Instead, he spent hours developing his piano technique.

By the time Ludwig was ten years old, his talent had attracted the attention of the elector. He decided to give Ludwig the best musical training available.

LUDWIG FINDS A TEACHER

Sometime during 1779 or 1780, Ludwig began studying with Christian Gottlob Neefe. Neefe, the court organist and a talented composer, recognized Ludwig's genius. He instructed Ludwig on the keyboard and gave him lessons in musical composition. In 1782, after much study, Ludwig became Neefe's assistant court organist. Within a year, Neefe left Ludwig in charge of directing the orchestra in his absence. This significant responsibility must have boosted the twelve-year-old's confidence enormously. In March 1783, Neefe wrote a glowing report about Ludwig in a music magazine:

> [Ludwig] van Beethoven, . . . [is] a boy of most promising talent. He plays the clavier [piano] most skillfully and reads at sight very well. . . . This youthful genius is deserving of help to enable him to travel. He would surely become a second Wolfgang Amadeus Mozart were he to continue as he has begun.

Ludwig took pride in his new status as a musician at the court. No longer dirty and poorly clothed, he wore an impressive outfit to court occasions. An observer described him as wearing a "sea green tail coat, short green knee britches, white or black silk hose, shoes with black bows, a white flowered silk waistcoat with flap pockets, the waistcoat bordered with pure gold cord, hair dressed in curls and pigtail, a cocked hat under his arm and a sword, carried also on the left, with a silver sword-belt."

About this time, Ludwig also began making friends. Helene von Breuning, a young widow, wanted to obtain a piano teacher for two of her children. Ludwig took the job, and soon he was spending most of his time in their household. In contrast to his own troubled family, the Breunings provided him with warmth and friendship. Many of the Breuning children became his companions for the rest of his life. Franz Wegeler, another young boy who enjoyed staying at the Breunings, also became Ludwig's great friend. Years later, Wegeler described how the Breunings gave Ludwig "the first happy discoveries of his youth. Beethoven was soon treated as a son of the house. Not only did he spend the greater part of the day there, but sometimes even the night. Here he felt himself free; here he could move about with ease; everything combined to make him cheerful and develop his intellect."

THE ENLIGHTENMENT COMES TO BONN

The Breunings introduced Ludwig to the writers and thinkers of Bonn society. Taking part in their conversations and debates, Ludwig was exposed to the new ideas sweeping through Europe. One of these intellectual movements, called the Enlightenment, influenced Ludwig for the rest of his life.

The philosophers of the Enlightenment believed that reason could free humankind from harsh laws and old superstitions. They believed that changes in political and social structures could lead to a society in which all people felt content and happy. The idea of reform, however, threatened the kings and queens of Europe. Most of them ruled their countries with few limits on their power. The Enlightenment also threatened many members of the nobility, or the class of people who owned most of the wealth and property in Europe. While most Europeans toiled in fields or in shops, the nobility owned palaces and lived off the income they earned from their land. They had little interest in changing the system that made them wealthy.

Not all European rulers rejected the ideas of the Enlightenment. Emperor Joseph II, who ascended the throne in Vienna in 1780, instituted bold reforms to make his kingdom more orderly, efficient, and prosperous. Bonn, which was part of Joseph's empire, soon felt the effects of his rule. In 1784, Joseph's brother, Maximilian Francis, became the elector of Bonn. To Ludwig van Beethoven and Neefe's joy, Maximilian shared his brother's beliefs. Bonn became a center of the Enlightenment in the region. Theater and opera were performed regularly. The ideas and art of great thinkers, such as Jean-Jacques Rousseau, Friedrich von Schiller, Johann Wolfgang von Goethe, and Immanuel Kant, were avidly discussed in the local university and library.

In this healthy atmosphere, Ludwig developed rapidly during his early teenage years. In 1784, Ludwig was officially appointed deputy court organist and received a modest salary. By the time he was sixteen, Ludwig's dazzling piano playing and musical ability won him many admirers. Such talent, they insisted, deserved the best training available, and they persuaded the elector to send Ludwig to Vienna. The magnificent city on the Danube River was seat of the Holy Roman Emperor

Joseph II's reforms included freedom of the press, religious tolerance, and tax relief.

and home to Europe's greatest musicians. The elector agreed, and in April 1787, Ludwig left Bonn for what promised to be the greatest journey of his life.

A TRAGIC DEATH

Instead, the journey proved to be a bitter disappointment. After spending less than two weeks in the city, Ludwig received a letter from his father demanding that he return to Bonn immediately. His mother, who had been ill with tuberculosis, was nearing death. Ludwig left Vienna and hurried home. "I found my mother still alive," he later wrote, "but in a wretched state of health." She died on July 17.

The death of Ludwig's mother thrust the seventeen-year-old into the position of head of the family. Mourning his wife's death, Johann

Did Beethoven Meet Mozart?

No one is sure whether Beethoven ever met the greatest musician of his age, Wolfgang Amadeus Mozart. One story recounts how Beethoven visited Mozart's Viennese apartment. When Mozart asked Beethoven to play, Beethoven began to improvise. Impressed, Mozart exclaimed, "Keep an eye on that one—someday he'll give the world something to talk about!" Most music historians, however, doubt that Mozart ever said such a thing. Beethoven may have met Mozart once or twice, but he had to rush back to Bonn before long. Mozart died in 1791, before Beethoven returned to Vienna.

sank deeper and deeper into the haze of alcohol abuse. Ludwig was forced to assume control of the family's finances and responsibility for his younger brothers and sisters. His one-year-old sister, Maria Margaretha, died that November. While these tragedies battered the family, Johann continued to drink heavily. Ludwig and his brothers often spent nights searching the streets of Bonn, looking for their father and then gently coaxing him home.

In late 1789, only a few years after his mother's death, Ludwig took firm action against Johann. He was worried that his father was wasting the family's money. Ludwig wrote a letter to the elector and requested that half his father's salary be transferred to him. Even more drastic, Ludwig asked that his father be banished from Bonn if he did not give the family a share of his pay. The elector, who was aware of Johann's drinking, agreed to Beethoven's request.

Ludwig turned to the elector of Bonn for help to prevent his father from spending his money on his drinking habit.

Now officially the head of the family, Ludwig van Beethoven supported his two brothers, Casper Carl and Nikolaus Johann, by becoming the court organist and playing viola in the court orchestra. Beethoven's participation in the orchestra exposed him to music written by Mozart, Franz Joseph Haydn, and other leading composers of the day. During the next two years, Beethoven composed several important works and increased his reputation for brilliant piano playing. In a musical newspaper, *Musikalische Correspondenz,* Carl Junker wrote, "I heard also one of the greatest of pianists—the dear, good [Beethoven]. One can, I think, judge this man from the wealth of ideas, from the highly personal expressiveness of his playing and the skill with which he plays. I do not know what he could lack in order to become a great artist. Even the members of this remarkable orchestra are his admirers, and all ears when he plays."

Viola

The viola is a musical instrument that is played on a lower range than the violin.

ANOTHER CHANCE TO GO TO VIENNA

In late spring 1792, the greatest composer in Europe, Franz Joseph Haydn, stopped briefly in Bonn. During Haydn's stay, Beethoven managed to show him one of his latest compositions, a piece written for a full orchestra and chorus. Haydn was impressed by the young man's work and suggested that Beethoven come to Vienna and study with him. Beethoven happily agreed. After weeks of preparation and packing, Beethoven left for Vienna in early November 1792.

Sitting in the horse-drawn coach that would carry him during the two-week journey, Beethoven carried a small album. On its pages, Beethoven's friends and supporters had inscribed letters of farewell, fond wishes, and notes urging him good luck. One note in particular, written by Count Ferdinand von Waldstein, was prophetic:

Dear Beethoven!

You are now going to Vienna in fulfillment of a wish that has so long been thwarted. The genius of Mozart still mourns and weeps for the death of its pupil. It has found a refuge in the inexhaustible Haydn, but no occupation; through him it desires once more to find a union with someone. Through your unceasing hard work, receive Mozart's spirit from the hands of Haydn.

Bonn, the 29th Oct. 1792

Your true friend Waldstein

Beethoven's father died less than a month later. Beethoven left no record of his reaction to the death, and he did not return to Bonn for the funeral. Although Beethoven did not know it at the time, he would never see his birth city again.

In Vienna, many members of royalty lived in grand palaces and sought musicians to entertain them.

TWO

City of Dreams and Music

Vienna, the capital of the Hapsburg Empire, was a center of power, wealth, culture, and music. Two musical geniuses of the age, Mozart and Haydn, had premiered their masterpieces in this city. The emperor's court constantly required new operas, masses, dances, and court music. It provided one of the greatest musical forums in Europe. The nobility, who maintained luxurious palaces throughout the city, demanded new music for their balls, rituals, and private pleasure.

A traveler to Vienna in the late 1800s reported that music was the only thing the nobility did well. "Many houses have their own band of musicians," he observed. "One can assemble four or five large orchestras, all of them unequaled." A Viennese citizen declared that "the nobility were probably the most musical that has ever existed. The whole population took part in the happy art, and their lively spirit, their sensual, pleasure-loving character demanded variety and cheerful music on all occasions."

A growing middle class of merchants, some wealthier than members of the nobility, also clamored for new music and musical instruction. More than three hundred pianists already lived in Vienna when Beethoven arrived there on November 10, 1792, but this competition did not discourage him. He possessed several letters of introduction from his friend Count Waldstein, which would gain him entrance to the houses of the nobility. He also had an invitation to study with the great Haydn. Most importantly, however, Beethoven had enormous confidence in his own genius.

LOVED BY THE ROYALS

Young, fiery, and brilliant, Beethoven exploded onto the Viennese music scene. In contrast to the delicate playing then fashionable in Vienna, Beethoven played the piano with passion, pounding out notes before abruptly shifting into soft, rippling passages of such beauty that his audience was left in tears. Many listeners were offended by Beethoven's style, but most were mesmerized. One listener remembers, "In whatever company, he knew how to produce such an effect upon every hearer that frequently not an eye remained dry, while many would break out into loud sobs; for there was something wonderful in his expression in addition to the beauty and originality of his ideas and his spirited style of rendering them." A rival pianist bitterly remarked, "Ah, he is no man, he is a devil. He will play me and all of us to death!"

Beethoven's style took advantage of recent innovations in the piano. The piano was invented in the early 1700s but did not become popular until after 1750. Until then, most people played the harpsichord. The harpsichord had a bright, crisp sound, but did not allow the player to control the volume. The piano solved this problem. The harder a pianist hit a piano key, the louder it sounded (The piano was originally called the pianoforte because it could be played both piano—softly—and forte—loudly.) The pianist could also hold a note much longer than he or she could on the harpsichord by simply holding down the key. These innovations, combined with a rounder tone, gave musicians new ways to convey emotion. Beethoven was one of the first musicians to exploit the piano's enormous range of sound.

An Instrument for Beethoven

Beethoven's musical skill attracted the attention of piano makers. Beethoven examined many pianofortes. Some he found too loud, some too soft. Some had a tone that was too dark or too light. Beethoven preferred the kind made by Johann Streicher, a piano maker who had settled in Vienna. Beethoven complained that many pianos sounded too dainty. "One often thinks one is merely listening to a harp," Beethoven wrote to Streicher in 1796. "And I am delighted that you are one of the few who realize that if one can feel the music, one can also make the pianoforte sing."

Beethoven was also a master of improvisation, or the act of composing music on the spur of the moment. Improvisation demanded that a musician play a tune out of his head, creating new melodies and harmonies as he went along. Of all musical skills, improvisation was regarded as the most difficult to master and the truest measure of musical genius. The musician must play the instrument like a person hums a new tune. Europe was filled with expert pianists, but only a few could improvise brilliantly.

A PROUD MUSICIAN

Portraits made of Beethoven in the first years after his arrival in Vienna show him looking confident and well-dressed. His broad forehead is framed by thick, brown hair. His mouth is firmly closed in an expression of determination. His eyes are dark and intense.

These pictures, however, don't show Beethoven's unrefined manner, coarse speech, and his often careless style of dress. Most of his wealthy listeners were well groomed and adorned in the latest fashions. Beethoven, however, sometimes appeared before his audiences with his hair sticking out in all directions. "He was small and plain-looking, with an ugly red, pockmarked face. His hair was quite dark and hung almost shaggily around his face," wrote one woman.

Sensitive and proud, Beethoven refused to defer to the nobility. At that time, most of the nobility considered musicians to be servants, like housekeepers, gardeners, and cooks. But Beethoven would not behave like a servant for his wealthy hosts. He could be rude and quarrelsome, and he was easily enraged. On more than one occasion, Beethoven shocked his noble audience by suddenly ceasing to play and stomping

This painting of Beethoven shows him to be intense and determined.

off in fury. This occurred at the slightest indication that his listeners were not paying full attention. He demanded their respect.

Beethoven's aloofness, arrogance, and rudeness only made the Viennese nobility admire him more. In a city where musical taste was eagerly cultivated, Beethoven's presence made his patrons feel culturally superior to their neighbors. Beethoven became the darling of the upper class, and several of them became his strongest supporters. Prince Karl Lichnowsky invited Beethoven to stay in his palace. He even told his servants that if both he and Beethoven rang for service at the same time, the servants should attend to Beethoven first! Lichnowsky and Beethoven became great friends, and Lichnowsky used his influence to further Beethoven's career.

BECOMING A COMPOSER

Although Beethoven's career as a pianist was a complete success, his education in composing was not. Within two weeks of his arrival in Vienna, Beethoven began studying with Haydn. But Beethoven soon felt that Haydn was distracted and not teaching him sufficiently. Beethoven secretly began learning composition with another teacher.

Around the same time, Beethoven's musical productivity declined. Perhaps he was troubled by the death of his father. Perhaps he was torn between his admiration for and jealousy of Haydn. In any case, he deceived Haydn and gave him "new" works that he had actually composed earlier in Bonn. Delighted with these compositions, Haydn wrote to the elector in Bonn, describing Beethoven as a good student and enclosing some of the "new" compositions. Haydn was shocked when the elector sent a sharp reply, informing Haydn that he had already heard the compositions performed in Bonn. The elector was furious, and Haydn was disappointed.

Beethoven's first compositions published in Vienna were three piano trios. Haydn admired the first two, but was baffled by the third, a stormy work written in the key of C minor. He suggested that Beethoven not publish it, a recommendation that infuriated Beethoven. The third trio was his favorite, and he suspected that Haydn was jealous of him.

Their relationship grew strained when Beethoven published a set of piano sonatas. While Beethoven did dedicate them to Haydn, he refused to put "pupil of Haydn" on the title page, a common practice at the time. Privately, Beethoven growled that Haydn never taught him a thing.

In January 1794, Haydn left for a concert tour in London and never taught Beethoven again. Later, the two appeared together in concerts. Although they were polite to each other, Beethoven held a grudge against Haydn for the rest of his life.

Joseph Haydn faced some challenges with his student Beethoven.

BEETHOVEN'S EARLY PERIOD

Whether Beethoven admitted it openly or not, Haydn was a central figure in the musical tradition he was now mastering. Composers did not just sit down and write music. They composed music that followed rules. Of course, all great composers altered these rules, which led to new developments and creations. Beethoven would eventually become one of the greatest rule-breakers in music history.

Beethoven scholars have divided his work into three periods: early, middle, and late. There is much disagreement over where these periods start and end, and some scholars reject the classification system altogether. Still, the three periods offer a broad structure to help people understand Beethoven's life and musical development.

In Beethoven's early period, which lasts roughly from 1795 to 1802, much of his music imitated the styles of Mozart and Haydn and other lesser-known composers. Beethoven's first published work was a set of piano trios. Beethoven gave the works a number—opus (op.) 1. Whenever Beethoven published a musical piece, he gave it an opus number (*opus*

Piano Trios and Sonatas

Beethoven's early compositions included piano trios and piano sonatas. A piano trio is a musical piece for a piano, violin, and cello. A piano sonata is only for the piano.

means "work" in Latin). Because Beethoven had already impressed the nobility with his piano performances, the Viennese eagerly purchased his compositions. Beethoven's first works were well received and made a handsome profit for both the publisher and the composer. His second published work, op. 2, consisted of three solo pieces for the piano.

From 1795 to 1799, Beethoven worked on a number of projects. He composed two concertos for piano and orchestra and six string quartets. In the late 1790s, Beethoven began composing a symphony, his most ambitious project yet. In his First Symphony, Beethoven followed a pattern. A Viennese symphony had four separate sections called movements. Following the tradition of the time, the first movement was bold and exciting. The second movement was slow and was followed by a minuet, or a light dance. A fast and lively fourth movement brought the symphony to a close. As with his quartets, Beethoven wanted to write a symphony that would compare favorably with the works of Haydn and Mozart. He did not fail, but his First Symphony was a cautious work. Beethoven was still understanding and developing his creative powers.

Musical Movements

The term movement is used to describe one section of a musical work.

LISTENING TO BEETHOVEN

Most people have heard some of Beethoven's works. Today, Beethoven's music is readily available on thousands of recordings that can be purchased in a store or online or borrowed from a local library.

At first, listening to Beethoven may be intimidating or strange, because his music bears little resemblance to the music commonly heard today on the radio and on television. Few people sing, and when they do, it's rarely in any language but German. However, Beethoven's music rewards repeated listenings.

Chamber Music

At first, Beethoven wrote music mostly for small groups of listeners. This music was played alone or by groups of friends, usually in homes. Chamber music takes its name from type of rooms in which it was performed. It was not intended for performance in large halls or on stages. There are several kinds of chamber music.

SONATA one instrument accompanied by piano (or the piano alone).

TRIO three instruments. A piano trio is for piano, violin, and cello.

QUARTET four instruments. Usually, a quartet is made up of string instruments, such as two violins, a viola, and a cello.

QUINTET five instruments. Like the string quartet, a quintet is usually made up of string instruments: two violins, two violas, and a cello.

PATHÉTIQUE AND MOONLIGHT

Beethoven gave the first true demonstration of his revolutionary genius on an instrument he had long been comfortable playing and composing for—the piano. Two piano sonatas, op. 13 and op. 27 no. 2, are classics today. But it is important to realize how new, even shocking, they sounded when they were first played in the music salons of Vienna.

The op. 13 sonata, called the *Sonate Pathétique,* opens with a booming chord and then develops into a slow, somber introduction marked Grave. This is the first time Beethoven used a slow opening in his piano sonatas. More important, the tragic tone of the opening dominates the piece, reappearing dramatically in the first movement and lingering behind the melodies and structures of the second and third movements.

Beethoven's *Moonlight* Sonata is one of his most recognizable pieces (though Beethoven did not think of the title). In the sonata, Beethoven was taking music in a new direction. He described the piece as partly a fantasy. In a fantasy, normal rules don't apply. His listeners would have expected the first movement to sound a certain way. But Beethoven gave them a quiet, dark, and repetitive opening movement. His listeners would have expected the first movement to be the most important in the sonata. Beethoven, however, saved the best for last. There is a third movement that explodes with extraordinary power, fury, and energy.

THE GROWING SILENCE

By the end of the 1700s, everything seemed to be going well with Beethoven's career. After arriving in Vienna as an unknown pianist from a small town, he was the favorite of the aristocracy. More important, Beethoven's creative powers were developing rapidly. Flush with confidence, Beethoven decided he would no longer perform any pieces in concert except ones he had written. Publishers eagerly bid for these works, and Beethoven earned a comfortable amount of money from their sale.

"I have six or seven publishers for every work, and more if I wish," Beethoven reported with delight to a friend. "They no longer bargain with me. I demand, they pay. You can see that it is a pleasant situation." Beginning in 1800, Beethoven also received a set amount of money each year from his friend Prince Lichnowsky.

Not everything was perfect, however. For several years, a sinister buzzing and ringing had been growing steadily louder in Beethoven's ears. At first, he tried to ignore it. Then he tried to treat it or explain it away. But by 1800, the noise threatened to crowd out all other sounds, and Beethoven was becoming frantic. Beethoven, a young man who aspired to become the greatest musician in Europe, was going deaf.

This is part of the score of *Moonlight* Sonata.

THREE

Crisis at Heiligenstadt

In July 1801, Beethoven wrote a letter to a friend, Karl Amenda. For the first time we know of, he admitted to someone that something was drastically wrong. "I wish that you were with me, for your Beethoven lives most unhappily," wrote Beethoven. "You must be told that the finest part of me, my hearing, has greatly deteriorated. . . . Oh, how happy I should be now if only I had the full use of my ears!"

By the time he wrote this letter, Beethoven was already struggling to understand normal conversation. To hear dialogue at the theater, he had to sit in the front row and lean toward the stage. Beethoven was devastated by the decline of his hearing and began to withdraw from society.

"I am leading a miserable life; for almost two years," he wrote to Franz Wegeler, "I have been avoiding all social functions, just because I find it impossible to tell people: 'I am deaf.'"

Despite this development, Beethoven could still write music. Like most composers, Beethoven could read music and "hear" notes in his head. He did not need a piano or any other instrument to help him compose. Beethoven's deafness, however, caused him to feel bitterly alone and misunderstood by his friends and patrons. For someone who relied on friendship as much as Beethoven did, the development was devastating.

He spent the summer of 1802 in Heiligenstadt, a small village north of Vienna. During the summer, Beethoven normally fled the city's heat and noise, and he hoped that the peaceful village would help him recover his hearing. For most of the summer, Beethoven worked on new

Beethoven came to this house in Heiligenstadt to escape the city and, he hoped, to restore his hearing.

compositions as he strolled through patches of woodland and farmland. He was very productive. He wrote two piano sonatas, three violin sonatas, and his Second Symphony. But his hearing did not improve, and Beethoven began to realize that his deafness might be incurable.

THE "HEILIGENSTADT TESTAMENT"

This shattering realization drove Beethoven to the brink of suicide. His music, his career, and his purpose in the world appeared to be destroyed. In October, he poured out his frustration, pain, and agony in an extraordinary document titled the "Heiligenstadt Testament." Beethoven addressed this letter—part will and part suicide note—to his two brothers, Caspar Carl and Nikolaus Johann, who were living in Vienna. But Beethoven not only wrote to his brothers, he cried out to the entire world. The letter begins, "O you men who believe or declare that I am malicious, stubborn . . . how greatly you wrong me!"

In the letter, Beethoven describes his pain. "I was yet compelled to isolate myself, to spend my life in solitude. . . . I could not say to people: 'speak louder, shout for I am deaf.'"

The letter also explains how his deafness crushed his ability to be friendly or socialize with others. "Therefore, you must forgive me if you see me draw back when I would gladly mingle with you. . . . I must live like an exile. When I do venture near some social gathering, I am seized with a burning terror, the fear that I may be placed in the dangerous position of having to reveal my condition."

The "Heiligenstadt Testament" is Beethoven's confrontation with his deafness and the cruel god, or fate, that caused it. The letter also

In the "Heiligenstadt Testament," Beethoven expressed his sorrow and anguish about becoming deaf.

represents a turning point in Beethoven's life. Despite the sobbing sentences and repeated cries for death, Beethoven is beginning to forge a new identity—an identity that comes to terms with his deafness. Several phrases in the "Heiligenstadt Testament" reveal this new attitude. Beethoven wrote, "Patience, they say, is what I must now choose for my guide, and I have done so." Beethoven also indicated a reason to keep living: "I might have easily ended my life. Only one thing, Art, held me back."

Over the next several years, Beethoven would use music to create a purpose for his life and to transform the tragedy of his deafness into victory. Beethoven did not go completely deaf for almost fifteen years. (Today, scholars are still unsure exactly why Beethoven went deaf.) Loud noises caused him great discomfort, but on some rare days, his hearing improved and he could understand spoken words.

Eventually, however, Beethoven was forced to give up public concerts and performances. He cursed his deafness for the rest of his life. But Beethoven never again surrendered to the despair that threatened him at Heiligenstadt. Instead, he returned to Vienna, and his next musical compositions showed a growth in scope and power. Nowhere is this more evident than in his next symphony—his third.

A NEW SYMPHONY

Beethoven worked on the giant project known as the *Eroica* Symphony during 1803–1804. He originally intended to dedicate the symphony to Napoleon Bonaparte, the leader of France. Napoleon had restored order in France after the bloody French Revolution. Like many Europeans, Beethoven admired Napoleon as a selfless hero who fought for the good of his people while respecting the revolution's ideals of liberty and freedom.

In 1804, however, Napoleon crowned himself emperor of France. The man who had originally sworn to protect his people had made himself their master. Beethoven exploded in rage when he heard the

Where was the "Heiligenstadt Testament" Kept?

Beethoven's "Heiligenstadt Testament" may not have been read by anyone while he was alive. It was only discovered after Beethoven's death. He had hidden it in a secret drawer in his desk.

Beethoven thought highly of Napoleon Bonaparte, the leader of France, until Napoleon made himself emperor of France.

news. "Is he [Napoleon] nothing more than human?" he shouted. "Now he will crush the rights of man. He will become a tyrant!"

Beethoven rushed upstairs and pulled out the symphony he had hoped to present to Napoleon. He erased Napoleon's name so violently from the dedication that he tore a hole through the paper.

THE *EROICA*

The *Eroica* Symphony is the musical journey of a hero through heroism, loss, and the joy of victory. The first movement begins with two crashing, defiant chords played by the entire orchestra. The first musical theme is played by the cellos, beginning an elaborate structure in which melodies are introduced, altered, and played again. The second movement is a tragic funeral march that expresses pain, bitter loss, and, finally, peace. Beethoven replaced the traditional dance movement with a scherzo, or a bright, upbeat section. The final movement is a theme and variations that ends with a triumphant mood.

For Beethoven, new musical innovations were needed to express human passion. The melodies and short phrases in *Eroica* are twisted, altered, and pitted against one another. They reappear in later movements and are played on different instruments. Sometimes, Beethoven changed the notes slightly, making a bold musical phrase suddenly sound tragic. Beethoven's creation was not simply a musical piece, but an emotional exploration of the human soul. It was nearly twice as long as any symphony written by Mozart or Haydn, and nobody had ever heard anything like it.

Music critics bitterly attacked the work. One complained that the symphony left the listener "crushed by a mass of unconnected and over-loaded ideas and a continuing tumult by all the instruments." Another observer noted that the symphony was "considered too long, elaborate, incomprehensible, and much too noisy." One musician simply called it "hare-brained."

Beethoven had grown emotionally stronger since his difficult summer in Heiligenstadt, so the fierce criticism he received did not

Special Elements of the *Eroica*

Beethoven's latest symphony featured many musical elements, including a scherzo and theme and variations. Scherzo is a fast and often humorous movement usually placed in a symphony. Theme and variations refers to a musical piece in which one melody (theme) is altered in several ways (variations).

discourage him. To a hostile review in a newspaper, Beethoven responded, "If you think you can injure me by publishing articles of that kind, you are very much mistaken. On the contrary, by so doing you bring your journal into disrepute."

Beethoven's Orchestra

The orchestra of Beethoven's time was smaller than but similar to the orchestra of today. It had several sections—a string section, a woodwind section, a brass section, and a percussion (drum) section. The string section was divided into first violins, second violins, violas (an instrument that plays lower than the violin does), cellos, and occasionally basses. The woodwind section was made up of flutes, bassoons, oboes, and clarinets. The brass section included horns, trombones, and trumpets. The percussion section was mainly large kettledrums and triangles.

Each of the instruments sounded different, even if they were playing the same notes. The flute and violin sounded bright and brilliant. The cello and bassoon sounded deep and dark. Beethoven used the instruments to convey a broad range of emotions and moods. As Beethoven grew older, he wrote music that demanded more instruments. Consequently, he expanded the size of the orchestra.

The Heroic Era

With the *Eroica,* Beethoven had brought music into a new era. Beethoven now began a period in which he produced a series of compositions of astonishing passion, originality, and beauty. His next two piano sonatas, the *Waldstein* and the *Appassionata*, are symphonies for the piano. Beethoven no longer limited himself to writing music that was playable by amateur musicians. The *Waldstein* Sonata has chords that explode up and down the keyboard, exploiting the full range of the instrument. The *Appassionata* Sonata alters its mood with incredible speed, suddenly changing both volume and rhythm.

Like the piano sonatas, Beethoven's next string quartets were giant works of fierce originality. Beethoven dedicated them to his patron, Count Andreas Razumovsky, who maintained an excellent string quartet

Beethoven used the French Revolution as the setting for his opera, *Fidelio*. While it was not popular at the time, the opera is still performed today.

at his palace. The music did not please its audience at first. They thought it was a joke. The cello player was so disturbed by the first quartet that he threw the music on the floor and angrily stomped on it. "Perhaps no work of Beethoven's met a more discouraging reception," a friend wrote later.

In 1804, Beethoven began writing his most ambitious work yet, an opera. The opera, entitled *Fidelio,* was set during the turbulent French Revolution. The heroine, Leonore, disguises herself as a man in order to enter a prison and save her jailed husband, Florestan. Leonore seduces the jailer's daughter to gain entrance to Florestan's cell. Pizzaro, the prison governor who is determined to kill Florestan, suddenly arrives and announces that Florestan will be shot. In the climax, Leonore, Florestan, and Pizzaro battle within the cell until a justice arrives and saves the day. The subject of this opera—a love story and a call for freedom—moved Beethoven deeply. They are reminiscent of his youthful passion for the ideals of the Enlightenment.

The opera's most beautiful scene involves Florestan removing his chains and embracing Leonore at last.

Unfortunately, the opera was a complete failure. As Beethoven prepared for the work's premier in November 1805, Napoleon's French armies invaded Austria and threatened to occupy Vienna. Most of the people who remained in the city could muster little enthusiasm for the piece. The critics, as usual, were harsh. In March 1806, Beethoven revised the opera and had it staged again. Again, it failed to inspire the public, and Beethoven was bitterly disappointed.

Beethoven experienced other public failures, too. He wrote his only violin concerto, a majestic work that combined dazzling violin playing with bold orchestral music. This work was also beyond the grasp of Beethoven's audience, and its first performance in December 1806 was received with little support beyond Beethoven's friends.

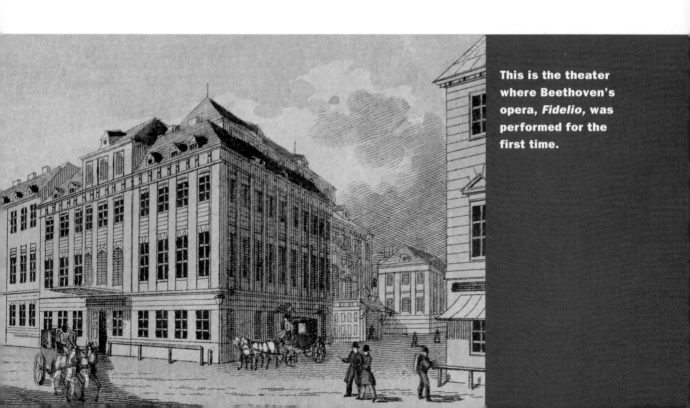

This is the theater where Beethoven's opera, *Fidelio*, was performed for the first time.

SOCIAL PROBLEMS

As Beethoven's deafness worsened, he desperately consulted doctors and underwent several cures in hope of regaining his hearing. To aid in conversation, Beethoven began using an elaborate "ear trumpet." The ear trumpet looked like a horn. Beethoven held the small end in his ear and asked his friends to speak in the larger end.

Unfortunately, the ear trumpets barely helped. Beethoven's friend from Bonn, Stephan von Breuning, describes how the deafness affected Beethoven's personality: "You would not believe what an indescribable and, I might say, ghastly effect the loss of hearing has had on him. Imagine

Orchestral Music

As Beethoven grew more popular, he wrote longer works for the stage and for concert halls. These pieces are grouped under the name "orchestral music," because they are intended to be played by large groups of musicians, such as an orchestra. Here are some examples of orchestral music:

SYMPHONY   A long piece written for an orchestra.

CONCERTO   A piece written for one or more solo instruments accompanied by an orchestra.

OPERA   A play in which most or all of the words are sung and accompanied by an orchestra.

what the feeling of being a victim can do to his [passionate] character—namely reserve, mistrust, often towards his best friends. . . . On the whole to be with him is truly an effort."

Unable to understand conversation, Beethoven often misinterpreted facial expressions and small gestures. He frequently suspected that he was the butt of a joke, and he lashed out in rage and frustration in response. Friends described him as a spoiled child who constantly threw tantrums.

Although Beethoven could be cold and irritable, he could also be tremendously warm and loving to those in his close circle of friends. And Beethoven's rage was often followed quickly by laughter. Many times, Beethoven would throw a friend out of his home, only to send notes that begged for forgiveness the next day. After a fight, he wrote a friend:

> Don't come to see me again! You are a treacherous dog.
>
> —Beethoven

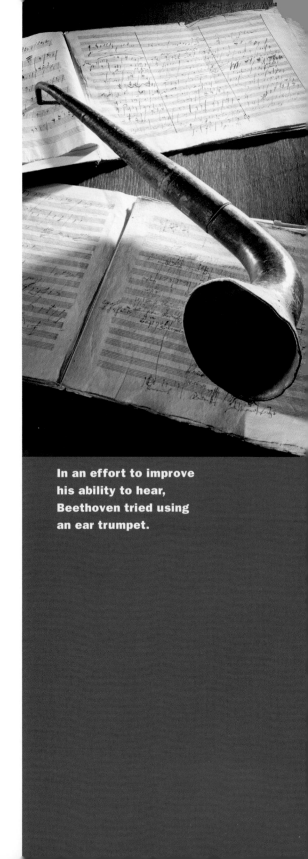

In an effort to improve his ability to hear, Beethoven tried using an ear trumpet.

The next day, he wrote:

You are an honest fellow and I can see now that you were in the right, so come and see me this afternoon.

A kiss from
Beethoven

Sometimes, however, Beethoven's quarrels were emotionally damaging to both parties and could not be so easily resolved. Beethoven had a painful falling out with Stephan von Breuning, his childhood friend from Bonn. In a letter to Ferdinand Ries, Beethoven wrote, "To Breuning I have nothing more to say. His manner of acting and thinking with regard to me proves that no friendly relationship should ever have been established between us and certainly will not be maintained in the future."

Beethoven was torn by the argument, and later he sent a heartfelt letter to von Breuning in the hope of making up. "Stephan! Forgive me if I hurt you; I suffered no less than you. When for such a long time I did not see you about me, I felt all the more clearly how dear you are to me."

Considering the passion Beethoven invested in his friendships, it is no surprise that his love life was a storm of emotions.

LOVE AND WAR

Beethoven frequently fell into and out of love. Ferdinand Ries remembered, "Beethoven was always glad to see women, especially beautiful, youthful faces, and usually when we walked past a rather attractive girl he would turn around to look at her again. He was very frequently in love, but usually only for a short time."

As early as 1794 or 1795, Beethoven had proposed to the singer Magdalena Willmann, who refused him because he was "ugly and half-crazy." In 1801, Beethoven wrote to his friend Franz Wegeler that he had met "a charming girl, who loves me and whom I love. At last after two years, there have been some moments of complete bliss, and this is the first time I have ever felt that marriage could make one happy. Unfortunately she is not of my social standing." Beethoven is most likely referring to Countess Giulietta Guicciardi, one of Beethoven's piano students (and sixteen or seventeen years of age) who flirted with him. But she also found Beethoven unattractive and refused his advances, a rejection that caused him great pain.

While Beethoven was not very handsome—his face was pock-marked and his features large—he could play music well. As has been demonstrated so often throughout history, good musicians are often very attractive to women. Beethoven was no exception.

"An inexpressible feeling that lies at the bottom of my soul has made me love you," wrote Countess Josephine von Deym to Beethoven. "Before I knew you, your music carried me away with enthusiasm for you. Your goodness of character and your fondness for me have done the rest." Beethoven pursued Countess Josephine, a widow with four children, in 1804 and 1805. However, she could not return his affection. Beethoven continued to press her, until she finally wrote him, "That I cannot satisfy [your] love, does this cause you anger?" Beethoven's interest in her ended the next year.

Beethoven's patron, Prince Lichnowsky, watched the fading of Beethoven's interest in Countess Josephine with relief. He had feared that she would damage Beethoven's creative output. But, as Lichnowsky discovered, Beethoven didn't break up with just his girlfriends, he also broke up with his regular friends. In autumn 1806, Beethoven stayed with Lichnowsky at his summer palace outside Vienna. One evening, Lichnowsky requested that Beethoven perform for some visiting French officers. Beethoven refused. He had no desire to play for the French, who were invaders in Austria. Lichnowsky insisted. After repeatedly demanding Beethoven's presence, the prince went upstairs, where Beethoven had locked himself in his room. Lichnowsky forced open the door to find Beethoven waiting to smash a chair over his head. Only the

Over the years, Prince Lichnowsky helped out Beethoven in many ways.

intervention of a friend prevented violence. Beethoven stormed out of the house into a pouring rainstorm. He returned to Vienna and smashed a bust of Prince Lichnowsky.

The next day, he dashed off a note to Lichnowsky. "Prince! What you are, you are by chance and by birth. What I am, I am by myself. There have been, there will be, thousands of princes. There is only one Beethoven."

Although Beethoven and Lichnowsky eventually rebuilt their friendship, the nasty quarrel left Beethoven without Lichnowsky's financial support.

WORK HABITS OF A GENIUS

Despite the chaos and turbulence in his personal life, Beethoven was amazingly productive and very disciplined when writing music. He began his day early with cups of strong coffee. A friend observed, "Beethoven rose every morning the year round at dawn and went directly to his desk. There he would work until two or three o'clock." Beethoven also spent several hours a day walking through the streets and parks of Vienna or in the farmland outside the city. When struck by a new melody or musical phrase, he dashed it down in notebooks that he always carried with him.

"I encountered Beethoven several times on my walks," wrote one observer. "It was most interesting to see him, a sheet of music paper and a stump of pencil in his hand, stop often as if listening, and then write a few notes on paper."

These notebooks are a fascinating record of how Beethoven composed. Many rough ideas and fragments for his symphonies, concertos, and chamber music appeared in his notebooks years before they were used in a musical score. Beethoven agonized over the best way to arrange the notes and he pursued perfection relentlessly. His notebooks include examples of the same theme developed in dozens of different ways. Even his scores are covered with angry slash marks, black blots of pen ink, and frazzled cross-outs.

Beethoven described his creative process to a friend:

I carry my ideas with me for a long time, and often for a very long time, before I write them down. In doing so, my memory is so trustworthy that I am sure I will not forget, even after a period of years, a theme I have once committed to memory. I change a great deal,

When Beethoven composed, he began by writing his ideas down in notebooks.

eliminating much and begin again, until I am satisfied with the result; then the working out, in extension, in diminution, in height and in depth begins in my head, and, since I know what I want, the basic idea never leaves me, it mounts and grows, I hear and see the work in my mind in its full proportions, as though already accomplished, and all that remains is the labour of writing it out.

In 1807 and 1808, after several years of writing and rewriting, Beethoven composed two new symphonies. As he had done with the *Eroica* Symphony, Beethoven gave his Viennese audience and the world something entirely new.

From Notebook to Musical Score

Beethoven first scribbled his ideas into notebooks. When he was ready to write the piece, he wrote out a full score. Often, however, Beethoven wasn't fully satisfied. The scores were full of corrections, scribbles, and cross-outs. Sometimes, entire pages had to be torn out and replaced. Then, a copyist had to make out Beethoven's scrawl and write out a clearer version. It was exhausting work. This version was then returned to Beethoven. Using a red crayon, Beethoven marked mistakes and indicated changes. The work was then returned to the copyist. Finally, the work was passed on to a publisher, who printed the music. Even then, however, Beethoven noticed mistakes. Furious, he once wrote to a publisher, "You are a mistake!"

THE FIFTH AND SIXTH SYMPHONIES

Beethoven's Fifth Symphony begins with the one of most famous musical phrases in history. Even today, its power shocks and electrifies audiences around the world. "Thus Fate knocks at the door!" Beethoven supposedly said to describe the opening phrase.

Beethoven does not use a melody as the basis for the work. Instead, he uses a short, simple musical phrase called a motif as the building block for the entire symphony. Through all four movements, this motif appears in different styles and moods. The first movement is thunderous and intense. In contrast, the second movement opens softly with a melody played by cellos and violas. This mood is broken by the "Fate" motif, which reappears at the beginning of the third movement. The third movement's terrifying mood is overwhelmed by the fourth movement—an explosion of joy and triumph.

The symphony spread through Europe, outraging some, provoking others to laugh in disbelief. But most couldn't resist the symphony's powerful vision. The famous composer Hector Berlioz wrote about the effect the symphony had on his teacher, who heard it for the first time in Paris. "I must get out into the air; it is astonishing, wonderful!" said the teacher. "It has excited and overcome me that in trying to put on my hat I could hardly find my head!" Once again, Beethoven had created something so new, so fundamentally different, that the music of Haydn and Mozart suddenly seemed centuries old.

If the Fifth Symphony expressed Beethoven's heroic spirit, the Sixth Symphony is Beethoven's tribute to nature. Beethoven took great delight in the peace of the countryside, and he looked forward to spending his summers in Heiligenstadt or other rural areas. He once wrote to a friend, "How delighted I should be to ramble for a while through bushes, woods, under trees, through grass and around rocks. No one can love the country as much as I do." Beethoven called his Sixth Symphony "Pastoral Symphony, or Recollections of Country Life."

Beethoven included small passages of text to explain what each movement of the symphony represented. The first movement begins softly and swells with emotion to evoke the "Pleasant, cheerful feelings aroused on approaching the countryside." Beethoven captures the mood of unrestrained, joyful anticipation. The second movement is a long and lazy "scene by a brook." The music portrays a soft, bubbling stream with birds, represented by flutes and piccolos, chirping in nearby trees. A "Jolly gathering of villagers" dance together in the third movement. A nearing thunderstorm

Beethoven's walks in this area of the countryside are said to have inspired his Sixth Symphony.

rumbles ominously. Suddenly, a violent thunderstorm explodes over-head in the fourth movement, scattering the dancing villagers. After a few terrifying minutes, the weather clears and a shepherd's song gives "Grateful thanks to the Almighty after the storm."

On December 22, 1808, Beethoven gave a concert that included the Fifth and Sixth Symphonies. The concert lasted more than four hours before the exhausted audience members made their way home in the winter chill. "You can have too much of a good thing," one member of the audience noted.

The Fifth and Sixth Symphonies were soon to be considered among the greatest works in the history of music. When listening to the Fifth Symphony, later generations would see Beethoven defiantly shaking his fist at fate. With this gesture, Beethoven changed the definition of the artist and laid the foundation for a new age of emotion and expression called the Romantic Era.

FIVE

Frustration and Invasion

In 1808 and 1809, Beethoven seriously considered leaving Vienna. "People should bear in mind that nobody in Vienna has more enemies than I have," he wrote to his publisher after the December concert. "This is more understandable since the state of music here is becoming worse and worse."

Beethoven had grown weary of not having a secure income. In 1808, he received an offer from a German state to become the court musician. The position paid well, and Beethoven debated whether to accept it. When Beethoven's friends and patrons discovered that he might leave Vienna, they frantically sought ways to keep him in the city.

Archduke Rudolph promised to help keep Beethoven in Vienna by giving a certain amount of money each year.

Prince Lobkowitz, Prince Kinsky, and Archduke Rudolph pledged to pay Beethoven a yearly salary. Their only condition was that he remain in Vienna. On March 1, 1809, Beethoven received a document that stated, "only one who is free from care . . . can create works of magnitude which are exalted and ennoble art. [We] have decided to place Herr Ludwig van Beethoven in a position where the necessities of life shall not . . . clog his powerful genius."

Beethoven was thrilled. Receiving an annual salary gave him independence and security that most musicians could only dream about. He wrote to a friend, "You will see from the enclosed document . . . how honorable my remaining here [in Vienna] has now become for me." Although he finally felt financially secure, Beethoven still yearned for a wife. Only half joking, Beethoven finished the letter, "Now you can help me look for a wife. Indeed you might find some beautiful girl at Freiburg where you are now, and one who would perhaps now and then grant a sigh to my harmonies."

In May 1809, French armies again invaded Austria and marched on Vienna. The emperor and nobility fled the city, and Beethoven took refuge with his brother, Caspar Carl, and his family. French artillerymen lobbed cannonballs into the city, and the noise of exploding shells forced Beethoven to cover his tender ears with pillows. He wrote a miserable letter to a publisher, describing the effect of the siege: "You are mistaken in assuming that I have been very well. . . . The whole course of events has affected both body and soul. . . . What a destructive, disorderly life I see and hear around me: nothing but drums, cannons, and human misery in every form."

Despite the French invasion, Beethoven completed a number of important pieces during this year—his Fifth Piano Concerto (called *The Emperor*), the Harp String Quartet, three piano sonatas, and several smaller works.

By 1810, Vienna again enjoyed peace. Beethoven, however, had no peace. He was in love again, this time with a nineteen-year-old woman

Beethoven Versus Napoleon

Beethoven had never forgiven Napoleon for making himself the emperor of France. When Napoleon led his armies against Vienna, Beethoven was especially enraged. Beethoven expressed his anger while composing his Fifth Piano Concerto. In the margins of the work, he scrawled "Song of Triumph for Combat! Attack! Victory!" Vienna fell, and Napoleon settled in the local palace. Beethoven, however, never met his former hero face to face.

named Therese Malfatti. Therese's parents, however, opposed the match, and she rejected Beethoven's offer of marriage.

Wounded once more, Beethoven retreated from love affairs for at least a year. He wrote to a friend while in despair, repeating his sorrow over his loss of hearing: "I should be happy, one of the happiest of people, if that fiend had not settled in my ears. . . . Oh, this life is indeed beautiful, but for me it is poisoned forever."

Beethoven's emotional swings, impatience, and fiery temper did not mellow with age. A friend complained, "Even among his oldest friends [Beethoven] must be humoured like a wayward child."

A SUCCESSION OF SERVANTS

If Beethoven was difficult with his oldest friends, he was nearly impossible with his servants. A continuous stream of housekeepers and cooks worked for Beethoven. Most of them quit. Others were fired by Beethoven for various reasons, both petty and serious. Some, he claimed, stole silverware. Others, he said, prepared soup that was too thin. Sometimes Beethoven broke open eggs that had just been purchased. If they were less than fresh, he angrily threw them at the servant who bought them. In his later years, Beethoven kept a diary that comically lists the comings and goings of his servants:

> April 17 the kitchen maid began her job
> April 19 a poor day [of service]
> May 16 fired the kitchen maid
> May 19 kitchen maid left

July 1 the kitchen maid began her job

July 28 the kitchen maid ran away in the evening

September 9 the girl began her job

October 22 the girl left

December 12 the kitchen maid began her job

December 18 the kitchen maid quit

Beethoven was a difficult man to work for because of his temperament and his messy ways. Many of his servants did not stay with him for very long.

Eventually, Beethoven had difficulty finding anyone willing to work for him.

Even with paid help, Beethoven existed in lodgings that were described as barely livable. A visitor to Beethoven's apartment discovered complete chaos. There were stacks of dirty dishes, piles of music, clothes strewn over chairs, rain puddles on the floor, tables covered with ink spills, and a piano shrouded in dust.

Beethoven was also restless, and he changed lodgings frequently. By the time of his death, Beethoven had lived in more than thirty locations in Vienna. According to a friend, "No sooner had he taken possession of a new dwelling place that he would find something objectionable about it, and would then run his feet sore trying to find another."

Beethoven's constant moving was one of the smallest annoyances he caused for his landlords. Besides being filthy, he played music whenever he was inspired, including late at night. Understandably, most of Beethoven's neighbors were relieved when he moved on.

FINANCIAL PROBLEMS

As Beethoven grew older, he became increasingly concerned about money. The 1809 arrangement that provided him with an annual salary soon fell apart. Prince Lobkowitz went bankrupt. Prince Kinsky was killed in a horse accident, and his heirs refused to fulfill his contract with Beethoven. Beethoven was forced to sue for the money in court. He later won the decision, but he was deprived of Kinsky's money for several years. The third noble who signed the contract, Archduke Rudolph, continued to satisfy his portion. However, this money was not enough.

Vienna's currency lost much of its value in 1811, and Beethoven panicked as his income appeared to be insufficient to cover his expenses.

Despite his financial worries, Beethoven composed two more works, the Seventh and Eighth Symphonies, during 1811 and 1812. In the Seventh Symphony, Beethoven uses dancelike melodies and sudden changes of tempo and speed to create excitement in the first and last

The Metronome

During most of Beethoven's life, there was no way to measure exactly how fast music should be played. Composers relied on terms, such as "allegro" (fast, lively) and "adagio" (slow), to tell musicians how fast they should play. However, a man named Johann Maelzel is credited with inventing a device called the metronome in the 1810s. (Dutch inventor Dietrich Winkel created a similar device around the same time.) The metronome kept a steady beat and could be adjusted to beat quickly or slowly. Beethoven was delighted with the metronome. Supposedly, he wrote the second movement of the Eighth Symphony as a tribute to the device. If you listen to the movement, you can hear the metronome beating time in the music.

movements. The second movement is the most famous part of the symphony. In this movement, Beethoven creates haunting passages out of a single note. In contrast to the serious Seventh Symphony, the Eighth Symphony is playful and fun. The slow movement is a comic joke, and Beethoven replaces the scherzo with the traditional minuet. The Eighth Symphony is Beethoven's salute to the symphonies of Mozart and Haydn.

THE MARRIAGE PROJECT

While composing his latest music, Beethoven continued to make preparations to marry. He wrote to a friend in Bonn, requesting a copy of his birth certificate (a person could not be married without one). Beethoven dreamed of finally escaping his loneliness by being surrounded by a loving wife and laughing children. Several biographers, including Maynard Solomon, have labeled Beethoven's actions during this period the "marriage project."

In 1812, Beethoven fell in love again. This time, however, his lover agreed to leave her husband and make her home with him. Beethoven's marriage project was on the verge of fulfillment. After all these years and so many rejections, Beethoven had finally found a woman who said yes.

Suddenly, however, Beethoven faced a new and difficult choice between the demands of his art and the potential demands of a family. In a heartbreaking letter, which he addressed to "The Immortal Beloved," Beethoven struggled to decide what choice he will make.

SIX

The Immortal Beloved

In 1812, Beethoven traveled to Teplitz (in the present-day Czech Republic) where he hoped to cure several nagging health problems. It was there that he wrote his famous letter to the "Immortal Beloved." Discovered after his death, this letter is Beethoven's most passionate expression of love. It begins:

July 6, in the morning
My angel, my all, my very self—Only a few words today. . . . Can our love endure except through sacrifices, through not demanding everything from each other; can you not change the fact that you are not wholly mine, I not wholly thine. . . . Love demands everything and that very justly—thus it is to me with you and to

you with me. . . . My heart is full of so many things to say to you—
there are moments when I feel that speech amounts to nothing at all—
Cheer up—remain my true, my only treasure, my all as I am yours.

After writing the above section of the letter, Beethoven returned to
it that evening:

Evening, Monday, July 6

Ah, wherever I am, you are with me—I will arrange with you
and me that I can live with you. What a life!!!!! thus!!!!! without
you. . . . I weep when I realize that you will not receive the first report
from me until Saturday—Much as you love me—I love you more—
But do not ever conceal yourself from me—Oh God—so near! so
far! Is not our love a heavenly structure, and also as firm as the vault
of heaven?

Beethoven then wrote that he must go to sleep. The next morning,
he added this last section.

Though still in bed, my thoughts go out to you, my Immortal
Beloved, now and then joyfully, then sadly, waiting to learn whether
or not fate will hear us—I can live only wholly with you or not at
all—Yes, I am resolved to wander so long away from you until I can
fly to your arms and say that I am really at home with you, and can
send my soul enwrapped in you into the land of the spirits. . . . No
one else can ever possess my heart—never—never—Oh God, why
must one be parted from one whom one so loves. And yet my life in

Vienna is now a wretched life—Your love makes me at once the happiest and the unhappiest of men. . . . Be calm—love me—today—yesterday—what tearful longings for you—you—you—my life—my all—farewell. Oh continue to love me—never misjudge the most faithful heart of your beloved.

> ever thine
>
> ever mine
>
> ever ours

WHO IS THE IMMORTAL BELOVED?

Beethoven's passion overwhelms him in the last section of the letter. Violent dashes separate the scrawled phrases. But the letter contains no woman's name, and the dates do not show the year. The letter has left Beethoven's biographers with a fascinating mystery. Who is the Immortal Beloved and why did Beethoven write her this letter?

Since the letter was discovered, Beethoven's biographers have named a number of possible candidates for the Immortal Beloved. In the last thirty years, Beethoven scholar and biographer Maynard Solomon has argued that Beethoven's Immortal Beloved was a woman named Antonie Brentano. Currently, Solomon's argument is accepted by most Beethoven scholars.

Antonie Brentano was born and raised in Vienna before she married merchant Franz Brentano on July 23, 1798. The newlyweds moved to Franz's home in Frankfurt, Germany. But Antonie desperately missed her life in Vienna, and she grew depressed. In autumn 1809, she and her husband returned to Vienna to nurse her ill father, who died on October 30.

To help his wife recover from her loss, Franz agreed to remain in Vienna for a longer period of time. Antonie met Beethoven in May 1810.

They began a friendship, and soon Beethoven was a regular visitor at the Brentano house. He played the piano for the family, and on some occasions he played with Antonie's children. No one is sure exactly when the love affair started. Solomon writes that it began in the fall of 1811. Earlier in the year, Antonie wrote a letter that already demonstrates how much she admired Beethoven. "He [Beethoven] walks god-like among mortals, his lofty attitude toward the lowly world and his sick digestion aggravate him only momentarily, because the Muse embraces him and presses him to her heart."

While it is still an issue up for debate, many historians agree that Antonie Brentano was Beethoven's "Immortal Beloved."

Throughout his life, Beethoven had suffered rejection in love. But Beethoven himself is responsible for many of his romantic failures. He frequently sought women who were married, above his social station, or too beautiful to consider him. In Antonie, Beethoven had at last found a woman who accepted and loved him. Beethoven's marriage project appeared complete.

It is this situation that makes the Immortal Beloved letter so tragic. Beethoven's writing indicates that Antonie has offered to leave her husband for him. But Beethoven cannot accept Antonie's offer. He cannot embrace the chaos a wife would cause to his life and his artistic work. The Immortal Beloved letter is a rejection, and Beethoven clumsily attempts to explain, "You forget so easily that I must live for me and for you."

But the letter, like Beethoven's stormy mood, passionately swings back and forth. At one point, Beethoven gives in: "I will arrange it . . . that I can live with you." But later he returns to his earlier feelings and rejects her again: "at my age I need a steady, quiet life—can that happen in our connection?" Beethoven closes the letter with fearful, even desperate requests that she still love him. "Love me—today—yesterday—Oh, continue to love me—never misjudge the most faithful heart of your beloved L."

There is no way to know whether Beethoven sent this letter. Perhaps he wrote this draft and then sent a different note. Perhaps Antonie, bitterly disappointed by the letter, returned it to Beethoven, who then locked it in a secret drawer in his desk along with his "Heiligenstadt Testament." In any case, the affair with Antonie failed. She returned to Frankfurt in the autumn of 1812. Though they continued to exchange friendly letters, Beethoven never saw her again.

BEETHOVEN FAILS AT LOVE

The end of this affair destroyed an illusion critically important to Beethoven's mental state, Solomon writes. To endure the tragedies of his life—his father's alcoholism, his artistic struggles, his deafness and loneliness—Beethoven had believed that one day he would find a true love. His letters often jokingly ask his friends to find him a wife. He pursued many women, seriously and playfully, for their affections, and his failures left him wounded but not hopeless. He wrote heroic music and he was determined to triumph in life.

Now, however, Beethoven began to face the reality of his existence. He was alone, and he realized that he would most likely be alone for the rest of his life. His marriage project had failed. His hope of finding peace in a wife and family was shattered. He wrote in his diary, "You may no longer be a man . . . for others. For thee there is no longer happiness except in thyself, in thy art."

The Musician and the Poet

In 1812, Beethoven met the greatest German poet of the age, Johann Wolfgang von Goethe. The two artists greatly admired each other. Goethe later wrote about his meeting with Beethoven: "His talent overwhelms me with admiration. But he is unfortunately an unruly personality, who is not wrong in finding the world detestable, but who does not make it any more pleasant for himself or for anyone else."

DARK MOODS, DARK DAYS

By mid-September 1812, the end of the affair with Antonie left Beethoven in a crushing depression. He soon directed his rage and sadness at other members of his family. In November, Beethoven visited his brother, Nikolaus Johann, in Linz, a city outside Vienna. To Beethoven's disgust and fury, he discovered that his brother was in love with his housekeeper. Beethoven demanded that Nikolaus Johann stop seeing her. Johann refused. The two argued so fiercely that they may have come to blows. Beethoven rushed to the local court and received a police order to banish the housekeeper. Infuriated by his brother's meddling, Nikolaus Johann married the girl, and Beethoven had no other choice but to return to Vienna in defeat.

Nikolaus Johann Beethoven rejected his brother's efforts to meddle in his personal affairs.

Beethoven's anger and stress were beginning to consume him. In December 1812, he wrote to a friend: "I have been ailing, although mentally . . . more than physically." In May 1813, Beethoven confided in a letter, "A number of unfortunate incidents occurring one after another have driven me into a state bordering on mental confusion."

Beethoven was on the verge of having a nervous breakdown. For the first time in nearly twenty years, his musical production ground to a halt. That summer, Beethoven's friends described his appearance with alarm: "He had neither a decent coat nor a whole shirt." Another

Beethoven's Private Thoughts

Twice in his life, Beethoven wrote regularly in a *tagebuch,* which translates literally to "day book." He is known to have kept one from 1812 to 1818. A *tagebuch* is not the same as a diary, in which people tend to record their impressions and feelings. Instead, Beethoven wrote down things that struck him, things that he wanted to remember. Some of the entries are about practical matters, such as how much money he spent on meals that month. Others are reminders, such as to buy black shoe polish because he expected visitors. Several entries are quotes from his favorite authors. They reflect Beethoven's attitude toward fate and fame. "Let me not sink into the dust inactive and inglorious, but first complete great things, of which future times also shall hear," Beethoven copied this passage from the *Iliad,* a famous Greek epic poem. A quote from another Greek poem struck Beethoven as worth remembering: "What greater thing can be given a man than fame and praise and immortality?"

observer noted that Beethoven sat at a table in an inn, where he was so filthy that diners avoided the tables around him.

POPULAR SUCCESS

Though deep in depression, Beethoven entered the period of his greatest success in Vienna. In late summer 1813, Beethoven was asked to write a composition celebrating the victory of the British general, the Duke of Wellington, over Napoleon, Austria's bitter enemy. Beethoven quickly composed a work called *Wellington's Victory,* which premiered in December 1813. The piece thrilled the Viennese, and Beethoven suddenly became the most popular composer in Austria. Encouraged by this success, Beethoven polished his opera *Fidelio* and staged it again. It took Vienna by storm.

In 1815, Napoleon and his armies were crushed at last, and a twenty-year period of warfare came to an end. Vienna was chosen to host a giant conference of the leaders of Europe. During the day, ambassadors and leaders debated new national boundaries and treaties. During the night, they entertained themselves at lavish balls and parties. Beethoven and his music were in demand.

Although Beethoven loved the attention, he knew that *Wellington's Victory* was far from his best work. He resented audiences for praising this piece when so much of his more important music was either mocked or ignored. Despite Beethoven's resentment, he was unable to compose anything other than shallow, patriotic music at this time. He was experiencing a major artistic crisis. The triumphant mood of his "heroic era," which had inspired the Fifth and Sixth Symphonies, the *Waldstein* Sonata, and the Fifth Piano Concerto, was no longer enough.

For the next several years, Beethoven's musical production fell off sharply. He looked inward for a new style of music that would express his recent tragic experiences and depression. Until he found this style, he composed very little. Beethoven suffered another series of blows during this period. His longtime friend and patron, Karl Lichnowsky, died in 1814. Another patron, Prince Lobkowitz, was bankrupt. Count Razumovsky's palace, where so many of Beethoven's works were originally played, burned to the ground.

A DEATH IN THE FAMILY

In November 1815, Beethoven's brother, Caspar Carl, grew very weak from tuberculosis. Beethoven kept watch at his bedside as his condition steadily deteriorated. In the final days of Caspar Carl's life, Beethoven convinced him to leave his son, Karl, in Beethoven's sole protection.

The Congress of Vienna brought together leaders from different parts of Europe. *Wellington's Victory* was warmly received by members of the congress.

Caspar Carl signed the will on November 14. But that same day, Caspar Carl must have realized that Beethoven intended to take Karl away from his mother, Johanna. Caspar Carl added a short paragraph that stated, "I by no means desire that Karl be taken away from his mother, but that he shall always . . . remain with his mother."

Caspar Carl anticipated the strife that would exist between Beethoven and Johanna. He closed his will with these words: "God permit them [Beethoven and Johanna] to be harmonious for the sake of the welfare of my child. This is the last wish of the dying husband and brother."

Tragically, Caspar Carl's words and wishes went unheeded. In the next decade, Karl became the object of Beethoven's fiercest affections and most bitter passions. The disastrous end to the Immortal Beloved affair had left Beethoven with almost no hope of having a family of his own. Suddenly, even as his brother sank into death, Beethoven saw a last chance at happiness. Beethoven's hopes and dreams settled on his brother's nine-year-old son, Karl.

Beethoven was determined to gain custody of his nephew Karl.

SEVEN

Beethoven and Karl

On December 20, 1815, Beethoven wrote to a court requesting that those parts of his brother's will that granted Johanna guardianship over Karl be overruled. Beethoven claimed that Johanna was morally and intellectually incapable of raising her own son. On January 9, 1816, the court accepted Beethoven's petition. Ten days later, Beethoven received the right to take custody of Karl. Beethoven wrote of his triumph to a friend: "I have fought a battle for the purpose of wresting a poor, unhappy child from the clutches of his unworthy mother, and I have won the day."

THE BATTLE FOR KARL

Karl was nine years old when Beethoven took him from his mother. Beethoven claimed that he was giving his nephew the opportunity to have a better life. But Beethoven's own words indicate that he was acting as much in his own interest as he was in Karl's. Disturbingly, Beethoven began to refer to himself as Karl's father. In his diary, he wrote, "You will regard K[arl] as your own child." In a letter to a friend, Beethoven wrote, "I am now the real physical father of my deceased brother's child."

While insisting that he was Karl's father, Beethoven also attacked Karl's mother, Johanna, with rage and bitterness. He claimed that she was immoral and a thief. He even accused Johanna of poisoning Caspar Carl. Beethoven's diary and letters are filled with wild accusations against her character.

Beethoven also felt guilty for separating Karl from his mother, and he arranged limited times for them to meet. This uneasy truce lasted a little more than two years. In June 1818, Beethoven discovered that Johanna had bribed his servant to give her information about Karl and had been meeting with him secretly. Beethoven was torn between his love for Karl and his fury at being betrayed by him. He violently confronted the boy. Beethoven later wrote to a friend, "[K]arl has done wrong, but—a mother—a mother—even a bad mother is still a mother." Beethoven's

Karl van Beethoven was caught in the middle of his uncle's custody battle with his mother.

words indicate his emotional confusion. He wanted to keep Karl for himself, and yet he acknowledged that "even a bad mother is still a mother."

Beethoven and Karl had a stormy relationship. On some occasions, Beethoven was loving and tender. On others, he was cruel and demanding. "My love for him [Karl] is gone," Beethoven once wrote to a friend. "He needed my love. I do not need his." Karl was not spared Beethoven's temper. Beethoven once wrote, "As long as I live he [Karl] shall never see me again, for he is a monster." However, Beethoven's anger always cooled, starting the cycle of constantly changing emotions once again. More often than not, Beethoven simply blamed Karl's mother for his problems with the boy. "All this confusion has made [Karl] stray from the right path," Beethoven stated, "and I even suspect that his mother may have made him swear to show me no marks of affection or love."

An Offer from London

Beethoven's music had grown extremely popular in England. In 1817, an orchestra, the Philharmonic Society of London, asked Beethoven to write two symphonies. They offered to pay him handsomely, and Beethoven accepted. The works were promised in four months. Beethoven, however, made some notes and then stopped composing. His artistic crisis and troubles with Karl had broken down his ability to compose.

KARL, LOST AND RETURNED

Johanna grew alarmed at Beethoven's treatment of her son, and she petitioned a court to have Karl placed in her protection. However, the court refused. In December 1818, Karl ran away to rejoin his mother. Johanna again applied to the court, and Beethoven turned to his powerful friends to get a favorable decision. Both Beethoven and Johanna testified before a judge. But Beethoven, who had claimed to be a noble, slipped up and revealed that he was not. Beethoven's case was thrown out of the high court and into the court for common people. In addition to this mortifying development, Beethoven received little sympathy from the new court. Karl was returned to his mother early in 1819. At that point, Beethoven became obsessed with separating Karl from his mother. "It is desirable," he wrote, "to make Karl realize that he is no longer to see such a vicious mother."

Realizing the intensity of Beethoven's obsession for Karl, Johanna petitioned the court to remove Beethoven as one of Karl's guardians. To Beethoven's horror, Johanna's petition was granted. Desperate, Beethoven considered kidnapping the child before his lawyer talked him out of it.

During the next months, Beethoven wrote letters to the court, asking that he again be granted legal guardianship of Karl. He acknowledged his past mistakes and pleaded for forgiveness. "Being human, I have erred now and then [and] my poor hearing must be taken into account, yet surely a child is not to be taken away from his father for those two reasons." In this letter, Beethoven again referred to himself as Karl's father. He also described his woes and attacked Johanna as a "monster of a mother." As a final touch, Beethoven wrote to the judge that not giving him Karl would "certainly cause the disapproval of our civilized world."

By writing "disapproval of our civilized world," Beethoven was reminding the judge that he had powerful friends in the court and aristocracy. The judge recognized Beethoven's hint and obeyed. Beethoven won his case, and Karl was returned to him for good in 1820.

BEETHOVEN'S BURDEN

Beethoven's obsession with Karl can be attributed to the enormous emotional upheaval then rocking his life. Beethoven had suffered the disastrous end of his Immortal Beloved affair. He was also writing very little music. During this crisis, Beethoven needed the young boy for companionship. Karl also offered Beethoven the fulfillment of one of his dreams—having a family of his own.

Beethoven's conflicting emotions and demanding love smothered the young boy. Karl was torn between obeying his uncle and loving his mother. Dragged from household to household and placed in court to testify against his own mother, Karl suffered tremendously. Few biographers defend Beethoven's obsessive rage against Johanna. It was possible that Beethoven was facing a crisis similar to the one he had faced at Heiligenstadt more than ten years earlier. He was almost completely deaf, and he no longer played music in public (although he still tried to conduct performances). In Karl, Beethoven hoped to find love, family, and a new purpose in life. Tragically, Beethoven's powerful needs were placed on the slender shoulders of a nine-year-old child.

After several years of turmoil and legal battles, however, Beethoven began to compose again. From 1812 to 1818, Beethoven had written few works. While he remained silent, Beethoven had undergone a profound change. As would soon be demonstrated, his music had reached new levels of mood, emotion, and maturity.

EIGHT

The Late Period

Beethoven's reputation in the city of Vienna changed during the years he struggled to make Karl his son. At one time, the Viennese people had tolerated Beethoven's tantrums and sloppy lifestyle as odd expressions of his genius. By 1820, however, most Viennese people believed Beethoven to be a lunatic.

HABITS OF AN OLDER ARTIST

In portraits made during this period, Beethoven appears intense and unconcerned with his appearance. His hair, now streaked with gray, is invariably unkempt and sticks out in all directions. His mouth appears locked in a frown. A contemporary described him as a hairy, growling bear.

In one incident, Beethoven wandered lost through a town. The local police, thinking him a tramp, arrested him and threw him into jail. After discovering that their prisoner was Beethoven, they released him with great apologies. Anton Schindler, Beethoven's friend and secretary during this period, described Beethoven: "His head, which was unusually large, was covered with long, bushy gray hair, which being always in a state of wild disorder, gave a certain wildness to his appearance."

Beethoven's bathing habits drew the attention of his neighbors. Standing naked in his room, he poured buckets of water over his head and sang or hummed at the top of his voice. The spectacle attracted people in the street, and Beethoven's servants often exploded with laughter when they caught sight of him. (Predictably, Beethoven did not think it was funny, and he fired several servants when he realized they were poking fun at him.) Beethoven's baths also bothered his downstairs neighbors. The water poured onto the floor and leaked into the apartment below.

After bathing, Beethoven walked through the streets of Vienna, locked in concentration. He hummed loudly and threw his arms about in wild gestures. Beethoven's appearance and actions attracted crowds, especially swarms

As he got older, Beethoven seemed to become more unusual in his ways.

of children who followed him, laughing, through the streets. Karl, then a teenager, was mortified.

By this time, Beethoven was almost completely deaf. To communicate, he carried several notebooks with him wherever he went. His conversation partner wrote in the book, and Beethoven answered aloud. (On some occasions, Beethoven answered in writing.) These notebooks, called conversation books, give intimate glimpses of Beethoven's daily life and record his thoughts on both trivial and important matters.

Although he was deaf, Beethoven stubbornly continued to conduct performances. In November 1822, an observer watched as Beethoven attempted to conduct a rehearsal: "With a bewildered face and unearthly inspired eyes, waving his baton back and forth with violent motion, Beethoven stood in the midst of the performing musicians and didn't hear a note! . . . The deaf master threw the singers and orchestra completely

Anton Schindler

As Beethoven grew older, he attracted a circle of admirers, most of them young men. Many of them would spend hours with Beethoven, helping him with clerical work and providing him with companionship. One member of this circle was Anton Schindler. Schindler would write the first major biography of Beethoven after the composer's death. Today, however, scholars distrust Schindler's biography. He is accused of stealing 140 conversation books and forging entries in them to make it appear that he and Beethoven were much closer than they actually were.

off the beat and into the greatest confusion." Finally, the orchestra stopped, and Beethoven looked around in bewilderment. Beethoven's friend, Anton Schindler, scribbled a note to Beethoven: "Please, let's leave now." Beethoven understood at once and fled to his home, where he collapsed on a couch and buried his face in his hands. Schindler later wrote, "He never wholly recovered from the effect of the blow."

COMPOSING AGAIN

In the late 1810s and early 1820s, Beethoven's brain seethed with ideas for new compositions. Beethoven began his new musical period (referred to as the Late Period by musical historians) by returning to the piano. Between 1818 and 1822, Beethoven composed several piano sonatas and other important piano pieces.

In these works, Beethoven begins to express a new style. In the *Hammerklavier* Sonata, he builds an entire movement out of a simple theme announced at the beginning. Through four movements, Beethoven wrote passages of enormous technical difficulty. "Now there you have a sonata that will keep the pianists busy for fifty years," he claimed.

He ends the piece with a gigantic fugue. Beethoven's use of a fugue recalls a musical age—the Baroque Era—before the Classical Age of Mozart, Haydn, and himself. The Classical Age had largely rejected fugues as too complex and ugly. Beethoven, however, now sought different musical forms in which to express himself. He discovered in older music possibilities that no one had ever considered. More than half of Beethoven's late pieces contain fugues.

In the three piano sonatas written after the *Hammerklavier* Sonata, Beethoven shows another characteristic of his Late Period—songlike lyricism. Lyricism refers to the long and tender melodies that appear in Beethoven's late works.

While composing these pieces, Beethoven played the notes with one hand while he pressed down several keys with the palm of his other hand. The result was an unintelligible mass of sound. Beethoven obviously could not hear his own notes, and he did not want anyone else to either.

Beethoven was now absorbed in his work. A publisher asked Beethoven to compose a piece, but Beethoven refused. "For some time past," he explained, "I have been carrying about with me the idea of three other great works. . . . These I must get rid of."

All was going well. By the end of 1822, he had completed *Missa Solemnis,* a giant work for a chorus and an orchestra that was set to religious text. He also composed several smaller works and began planning a string quartet. Most important, Beethoven was making progress on a grand new symphony.

Fugue

A fugue is a musical piece in which one or more themes are repeated and interwoven together.

THE NINTH SYMPHONY

Beethoven had composed his Eighth Symphony in 1812. Ten years later, he wrote feverishly to complete his Ninth. In his sketchbooks, Beethoven worked patiently and exhaustively, reworking the phrases until they were perfect. Finally, they were incorporated into his final score.

News that Beethoven was composing a symphony soon reached his friends. Eagerly, they awaited the moment when it would be played. But Beethoven, disgusted with the Viennese people and their attitude toward most of his music, had promised the symphony to admirers in London. Beethoven's friends desperately tried to convince the composer to give Vienna the honor of hearing his newest symphony for the first time. Thirty musicians wrote him an appeal: "We know that a new flower glows in [the group] of your glorious, still unequaled symphonies. . . . Do not longer disappoint the public who waits!" Beethoven was very moved by the appeal, and he agreed to a concert date.

On May 7, 1824, a large crowd packed into the Kärntnertor Theatre in Vienna. A large orchestra and a chorus performed parts of Beethoven's *Missa Solemnis* and a smaller work. The Ninth Symphony was saved for last.

Beethoven's Ninth Symphony was performed here in 1824. The crowd loved his new work.

The symphony opens quietly, with violins playing a short musical phrase. As he did in the Fifth Symphony, Beethoven uses this phrase as the building block for the rest of the work. The second movement is a gigantic scherzo punctuated with the thunderous pounding of kettledrums. The third movement is slow, gorgeous, and passionate. It ends with a sudden, shocking chord that announces the fourth movement. Beethoven replays themes from the first three movements and then dismisses them, as if they are insufficient to express what comes next. After these three magnificent movements, the listener also wonders what could come next. Beethoven has recognized this problem. In the fourth movement, Beethoven turns to an instrument he has never used before in a symphony—the human voice.

After a tumultuous introduction, a male voice suddenly sings, "Friends! . . . Let us sing more cheerful songs, more full of joy!" That "song," of which Beethoven wrote more than two hundred versions before including it in the score, is the climactic melody of Beethoven's Ninth Symphony. Beethoven took the text from a poem written by the German poet Friedrich von Schiller titled "Ode to Joy." With these words, Beethoven returns to the Enlightenment ideals of his youth. He imagines a perfect society in which all people are free, happy, and at peace. "All men become brothers! . . . You millions, I embrace you. This kiss is for the entire world!"

The chorus sang, and the symphony swelled to its climax. At the sound of the last note, the theater exploded with applause and cheers. Beethoven sat with his back toward the audience, unaware of the reaction. A singer tugged his arm gently and turned him toward the cheering crowd. His turning around suddenly reminded everyone that Beethoven was deaf. The realization, one observer wrote, "acted like an electric shock on all present, and a volcanic explosion of sympathy and admiration followed, which was repeated again and again, and it seemed as if it would never end." The deaf composer bowed. It was one of his most successful concerts in Vienna.

As with so many of Beethoven's other works, not everyone was impressed with the Ninth Symphony. One writer explained the symphony as the mad ravings of a composer unable to hear his own music. John Ruskin, the English poet and critic, wrote, "Beethoven always sounds to me like the upsetting of bags of nails, with here and there a dropped hammer."

Critics also blasted Beethoven's use of voice in the fourth movement. One wrote with disgust that the fourth movement opened with "a common-place theme, very much like 'Yankee Doodle.'" Another cried, "But oh, the unspeakable cheapness of the chief tune!" One music historian has suggested that Beethoven's true fulfillment of the Ninth Symphony came later, in music he composed for a small, intimate musical group—the string quartet.

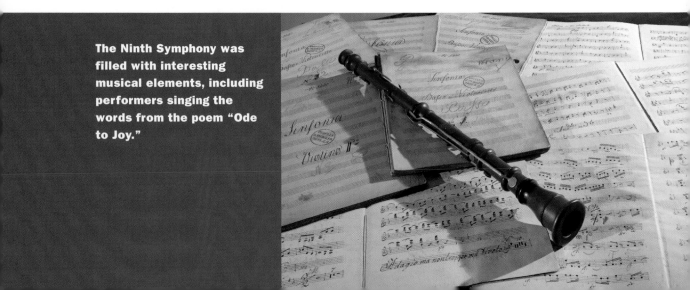

The Ninth Symphony was filled with interesting musical elements, including performers singing the words from the poem "Ode to Joy."

A NEW COMMISSION

In November 1822, Beethoven was excited to receive a letter from Nikolai Galitzin, a Russian prince. "As a passionate music lover, I am a great admirer of your talent," he wrote. "I write to you to ask if you would consent to compose one, two, or three new string quartets.

Beethoven was delighted by the prince's request, and he also needed the money. The concert for the Ninth Symphony was a success, but the ticket sales were not as great as Beethoven had expected. He nearly fainted with horror when he received the receipts. During a second performance, only half of the theater's seats were filled. Disappointed, Beethoven turned his full attention to composing the string quartets.

The works would occupy him for the last two years of his life. It is his last music, and many people believe it is the greatest music ever written.

THE LATE STRING QUARTETS

While Beethoven's last symphony expresses his heroic ideal, his last string quartets turn inward to explore the soul. Beethoven became entranced with composing string quartets. Although Prince Galitzin had requested three or fewer, Beethoven composed five. Each one has a different length and mood. These pieces contain some of Beethoven's most radical and original music.

The second quartet, op. 132, has five movements. While composing this quartet in April 1825, Beethoven fell seriously ill. Upon recovering from the illness, Beethoven wrote a movement he described as a "thankful song upon the return to health." The movement forms the heart of the op. 132 quartet. To write it, Beethoven imitated a style from the Middle Ages. The style was used in church services and evokes a deep sense of peace. Beethoven also wrote passages he labeled as "returning strength." These passages resound with joy and then return to the calm hymn.

After living a passionate life, after writing music in which he tried to defeat his hearing impairment in an explosion of sound, Beethoven seems to have moved on. He is no longer the hero fighting a battle. In simple terms, he may have learned to accept his deafness. In doing so, his music became even richer, and he wrote works that have never been equaled.

Beethoven composed the next quartet, op. 130, from July to December. It is a gigantic work made up of six movements. At the end of the quartet, Beethoven included a giant fugue of such originality, daring, and brilliance, that it still baffles modern listeners. When a friend reported that the quartet had not been well received by its first audience, Beethoven merely shrugged. "They will like it, one of these days."

As Beethoven began to work on his last two quartets in 1826, his family situation again intruded.

KARL TRIES TO TAKE HIS OWN LIFE

To Beethoven's relief, his relationship with Karl was peaceful during the first years of the 1820s. The boy spent most of his time at boarding schools. On holidays and weekends, and during summers, Karl lived with Beethoven and performed minor secretarial tasks.

Beethoven tried making up with Johanna. In late 1823, Beethoven heard that Johanna was suffering from an illness and had difficulty paying for her medicine. Beethoven wrote to her doctor and covered Johanna's debts: "I am sending her [money] . . . Please have it delivered to her through the doctor and, what is more, in such a way that she will not know where it came from." In January 1824, Beethoven allowed Johanna to keep the money she contributed every year for Karl's education.

This peaceful period did not last. After spending much of the summer of 1824 away, Karl reappeared on Beethoven's doorstep with a friend. Beethoven was still possessive of Karl and did not like Karl's new friend. "I think he is coarse and vulgar. Persons of that kind are not fit to be your friend," Beethoven wrote in a conversation book. Karl fired back: "If you think he is coarse, then you are mistaken. . . . Besides, I have no intention of exchanging him for another friend." The arguments between Beethoven and Karl grew so bitter that yet another housekeeper quit.

Beethoven also discovered that Karl had again started secretly visiting his mother. "Am I to experience once more the most horrible ingratitude?" Beethoven scrawled furiously into a conversation book to Karl. "My dream is to get away completely from you and . . . that horrible family who have been thrust upon me." Within a few weeks, Beethoven's mood had swung again. He wrote to Karl, "I embrace you. Be my good, hardworking, noble son as I am always your faithful father."

When Karl returned to school in the autumn, Beethoven sent him letters. Some begged his attention and demanded his love. Other letters were harsh and critical. In October, Beethoven wrote to Karl's teacher. Beethoven was suspicious that Karl was mixing with people from the wrong crowd. He asked Karl's teacher to keep him in at night. Karl exploded at this latest restriction and wrote a letter to Beethoven. It is unclear what the letter said (some historians claim that Karl threatened to commit suicide), but Beethoven pleads in his reply for Karl not to despair. "My beloved son! Stop, no further. Only come to my arms, you won't hear a single hard word. For God's sake, do not abandon yourself to misery."

Beethoven continued to control Karl's life. He demanded reports from Karl's teachers about where and with whom he was spending time. Desperate, Karl tried to free himself from Beethoven's crushing embrace. In late spring of 1826, the two quarreled so violently that Karl struck Beethoven and then fled.

On July 30, Karl left Vienna, sold his watch, and purchased two pistols. He wrote two suicide notes—one to Beethoven and one to his teacher—and shot himself in the head. The bullet just scraped his scalp, leaving him with a minor wound. Very alive, he asked that he be returned to his mother.

Karl's attempted suicide drew the attention of the local authorities. Karl reported to the police that Beethoven "tormented him too much" and that he was "weary of imprisonment." Beethoven was shocked by Karl's act, and he finally realized that their separation was unavoidable. With the help of Beethoven's friends, Karl secured a position in an army regiment and began a career in the military.

"IT MUST BE!"

Karl's attempted suicide shattered Beethoven, leaving him weary and depressed. A friend reported that Beethoven suddenly looked fifteen years older. Beethoven had also been suffering from poor health for several years, and Karl's attempted suicide robbed him of much of his remaining energy. Burdened by this emotional stress, Beethoven struggled to complete his last two quartets.

His op. 131 quartet consists of seven movements that are played without a pause. Beethoven called it the greatest piece of music he had ever written.

In Beethoven's last quartet, op. 135, he returned to the Classical four-movement style. He added revealing text to the last movement. Over three notes he wrote the words, "Must it be?" He answers triumphantly, "It must be!"

We are not sure whether Beethoven meant this to be a joke. Or, perhaps by asking "Must it be?" Beethoven was again wondering about fate and whether things must be the way they are. When writing the Fifth Symphony, he was determined to rise heroically above his miserable situation, to "seize fate by the throat." In this piece, Beethoven appears to be poking fun at himself. More than twenty years later, Beethoven had found a new peace with both the world and his place in it. Finally, he could answer with a smile and a wink, "It must be!"

THE FINAL DAYS

By December 1826, Beethoven's health was rapidly failing, and it became clear that he was dying. Beethoven's doctor reported that Beethoven trembled with shivers and bent over double because of the pain in his liver and intestines. His feet swelled dramatically.

News of Beethoven's illness spread, and friends began gathering to say their final good-byes. Through January and February 1827, Beethoven remained in his bed. At one point he cried, "Here I have been lying for four months! One must at last lose patience!" During this long period, Beethoven spoke with friends and recalled memories of his childhood. On March 23, Beethoven completed his will, leaving his entire estate to Karl and his descendants. After signing his name, he exclaimed, "There! I won't write another word."

On March 24, Beethoven slipped into a coma. Two days later, his breathing became shallow. On the afternoon of March 26, a thunderstorm appeared in the skies over Vienna. As the thunder crashed overhead, Beethoven suddenly opened his eyes and raised a clenched fist. It was his last gesture. The hand dropped, and Beethoven was dead.

Beethoven's funeral was one of the largest Vienna had ever seen. Schools were closed, and soldiers were called in to keep order. Thousands of people jammed together to see Beethoven's coffin as the funeral procession wound slowly through the city's streets to a village churchyard. Part of the funeral oration, written by the German poet Franz Grillparzer said:

He withdrew from his fellow-men after he had given them every-thing and had received nothing in return. He remained alone

What Happened to Karl?

Karl apparently lived a normal life after Beethoven's death. He married and had four daughters and one son. He named the son "Ludwig." Karl died in 1858 at the age of fifty-two.

because he found no second self. But until his death he preserved a human heart for all men, a father's heart for his own people, the whole world.

Thus he was, thus he died, thus he will live to the end of time!

Crowds gathered to say good-bye to Beethoven as his funeral procession traveled through the city.

Many composers, including Richard Wagner, were inspired by Beethoven's work.

NINE

Beethoven's Legacy

Beethoven left behind a staggering amount of music. He had composed nine symphonies, seven concertos, sixteen string quartets, an opera, six piano trios, ten sonatas for violin and piano, five sonatas for cello and piano, one sonata for horn and piano, twenty-one sets of piano variations, thirty-two piano sonatas, and a number of other works. It was not, however, just the amount of music he wrote that makes him so admired. He created a style of music no one had heard before that is still being played today.

Beethoven changed music and the way people listened to it forever. Beethoven's attitude also influenced how later artists acted, not just the art they produced. His defensiveness and independence, his constant declarations that he was serving his art, his disregard of the nobility—all

Beethoven continues to inspire millions with his work, which is performed in concert halls across the world.

of these characteristics were cherished by the next generation of artists. The great Romantic composer Richard Wagner described how he felt after hearing Beethoven's Seventh Symphony: "The effect on me was indescribable. I soon conceived an image of him in my mind as a . . . unique supernatural being."

Beethoven's influence on later musicians is incalculable. His stature as an artist was so enormous that later generations of composers openly admitted their inability to surpass his artistic achievements. Johannes Brahms, the great composer, struggled to escape Beethoven's shadow more than thirty years after Beethoven's death. When critics crowned him the successor to Beethoven, Brahms grew so terrified by the expectations placed on him that he put off writing his first symphony for decades. After years of agonizing toil, Brahms produced his Symphony #1. Unfortunately for Brahms, critics quickly dubbed the work "Beethoven's Tenth."

A Final Resting Place of Honor

Beethoven was originally buried in Währing Cemetery. His tombstone was decorated with a golden harp. His body remained there until 1888, when it was moved to a place of honor in a new central cemetery. He is buried there today, next to another great Viennese musician, Franz Schubert.

A CULTURAL ICON

Even today, Beethoven's scowl and enormous brow locked in concentration is part of popular culture. His life, his artistic struggles, and his relationship with his nephew have been the subject of several films.

Beethoven is part of an elite group of musicians whose work never goes out of style. People continue to crowd concert halls whenever Beethoven's music is played. There is little doubt that the music of this extraordinary genius will continue to be heard for as long as there are musical instruments and people to play them.

An Olympic Moment

Beethoven's music has united the entire world. On February 6, 1998, parts of the Ninth Symphony were played during the opening of the XVIII Winter Olympics. Via satellite transmissions and thousands of miles of wiring, five choruses on five separate continents sang together.

Timeline

1796 Beethoven publishes three piano sonatas (op. 2).

1799 Beethoven completes his First Symphony.

1802 In April, Beethoven moves to Heiligenstadt in an attempt to help his hearing. In October, Beethoven writes the "Heiligenstadt Testament."

1803 Beethoven composes the *Eroica* Symphony and the *Waldstein* Sonata.

1804 In May, Beethoven learns that Napoleon has crowned himself emperor of France. In a rage Beethoven erases Napoleon's name from the dedication of the *Eroica* Symphony. Beethoven begins composing an opera, *Fidelio*.

1805 Beethoven's *Fidelio* premiers and fails.

The French army occupies Vienna in November.

1806 Beethoven completes his only violin concerto. In late October, Beethoven quarrels with his patron, Prince Lichnowsky.

1807–1808 Beethoven composes the Fifth and Sixth Symphonies.

1811–1812 Beethoven composes his Seventh and Eighth Symphonies.

1812 The War of 1812 begins between the United States and Britain.

1813 Beethoven writes *Wellington's Victory*, which catapults him to popular fame in Vienna.

1814 Beethoven revises *Fidelio* and stages it to great success.

1814–1815 The Congress of Vienna, a meeting of several European leaders, is held.

1815 In November, Beethoven convinces his dying brother to give him custody of his son, Karl. Beethoven appeals to a court to place Karl under his exclusive guardianship.

Wellington defeats Napoleon at Waterloo. The War of 1812 ends.

1816 In January, the court rules in Beethoven's favor.

1819 Karl is returned to his mother. Beethoven writes several petitions for custody to the court, but they are rejected.

1820 Karl is transferred back to Beethoven.

1821 Beethoven continues composing several piano works and completes the *Missa Solemnis.*

1822 Beethoven tries to conduct a performance of *Fidelio,* but his deafness makes it impossible. Beethoven receives an offer from a Russian prince to write a number of string quartets.

1823 Beethoven begins writing the Ninth Symphony.

1824 Beethoven completes the Ninth Symphony and begins composing several string quartets.

1826 Karl attempts suicide. Beethoven completes his last quartets and falls seriously ill in December.

1827 Karl leaves for military service, and Beethoven's illness worsens. Beethoven dies on March 26 during a sudden thunderstorm and is buried three days later in a funeral attended by thousands.

To Find Out More

BOOKS

Autexier, Philippe. *Beethoven: The Composer as Hero.* New York: Harry N. Abrams, Inc. 1992.

Cooper, Barry, ed. *The Beethoven Compendium: A Guide to Beethoven's Life and Music.* London: Thames and Hudson, 1996.

Haas, Karl. *Inside Music: How to Understand, Listen to, and Enjoy Good Music.* New York: Anchor Books, 1984.

Hamburger, Michael, ed. *Beethoven: Letters, Journals, and Conversations.* New York: Thames and Hudson, 1992.

Hurwitz, David. *Beethoven or Bust: A Practical Guide to Understanding and Listening to Great Music.* New York: Anchor Books, 1992.

Kerman, Joseph and Alan Tyson. *The New Grove Beethoven.* New York: W.W. Norton and Company, 1997.

Landon, H.C. Robbins, ed. *Beethoven: His Life, Work and World.* London: Thames and Hudson, 2000.

ORGANIZATIONS AND ONLINE SITES

Beethoven
http://www.geocities.com/Vienna/Strasse/3732/

This site provides an in-depth look at Beethoven's life and work.

Beethoven the Immortal
http://magic.hofstra.edu:7003/immortal/index.html

This site is an excellent resource for general information on Beethoven's life and attitude toward performing, music, and life.

Beethoven-Haus Bonn Museum
http://www.beethoven-haus-bonn.de

Click on the British flag for an English language version of information from the museum at Beethoven's birthplace.

Ludwig van Beethoven
http://www.classical.net/music/comp.lst/beethovn.html

This brief site contains several links on a variety of topics, including several lists of suggested recordings.

Ludwig van Beethoven—Piano Sonatas: An Overview of Selected Recordings
http://www.classical.net/music/comp.lst/articles/beethoven/psonatas.html

Want to listen to some of Beethoven piano sonatas? This site gives an in-depth critique of what's available.

A Note on Sources

The most detailed and interesting book recently published on Beethoven is Maynard Solomon's *Beethoven*. I owe my interpretations of both the "Heiligenstadt Testament" and the Immortal Beloved letter to his biography. However, this book is probably too complex for most young readers. For a simple, well-illustrated look at Beethoven's life, look for Phillippe Autexier's *Beethoven: The Composer as Hero*. A more complex but lucid presentation of Beethoven's life is offered in The New Grove Beethoven. For a more controversial account of Beethoven's emotional growth through his music, see *Beethoven: His Spiritual Development*.

Beethoven's friends, enemies, and indifferent observers left a wealth of contemporary observations of him. These have been collected in a wonderful book, *Beethoven: His Life, Work and World,* edited by H.C. Robbins Landon. Michael Hamburger's *Beethoven: Letters, Journals, and Conversations* provides a similar collection, detailing Beethoven's life through his own words and the words of his contemporaries.

The complex subject of music theory and practice is clearly explained in Karl Haas's *Inside Music: How to Understand, Listen to, and*

Enjoy Good Music and David Hurwitz's *Beethoven or Bust: A Practical Guide to Understanding and Listening to Great Music.* Both titles have chapters on Beethoven's music and his impact on later generations of musical artists.

—*Brendan January*

Index

About the Author

Brendan January was born and raised in Pleasantville, New York. He earned a B.A. in history and English from Haverford College and an M.A. in Journalism from Columbia University. He is a Fulbright Scholar and an award-winning author of more than thirty books for young readers. Mr. January lives with his wife and daughter in New Jersey.